H **www.heinemann.co.uk/library**
Visit our website to find out more information about **Heinemann Library** books.

To order:
☎ Phone 44 (0) 1865 888066
🗎 Send a fax to 44 (0) 1865 314091
💻 Visit the Heinemann Bookshop at www.heinemann.co.uk/library to browse our catalogue and order online.

First published in Great Britain by Heinemann Library, Halley Court, Jordan Hill, Oxford OX2 8EJ, part of Harcourt Education.
Heinemann is a registered trademark of Harcourt Education Ltd.

Editorial: Jilly Attwood and Kate Bellamy
Design: Ron Kamen and Celia Jones
Photographer: Debbie Rowe
Picture Research: Maria Joannou
Production: Séverine Ribierre

Originated by Ambassador Litho Ltd
Printed and bound in China by South China Printing Company

ISBN 0 431 11936 8
09 08 07 06 05
10 9 8 7 6 5 4 3 2 1

British Library Cataloguing in Publication Data

Parker, Victoria
 We're From Japan
 952'.05

A full catalogue record for this book is available from the British Library.

Acknowledgements

Corbis/Royalty Free pp. **4a**, **4b**, **12**, **28**; Getty Images/Photodisc pp. **30a**, **30c**; Debbie Rowe pp. **1**, **5a**, **5b**, **6a**, **6b**, **7a**, **7b**, **8a**, **8b**, **9a**, **9b**, **10a**, **10b**, **11**, **13a**, **13b**, **14a**, **14b**, **15**, **16**, **17a**, **17b**, **18a**, **18b**, **19**, **20**, **21a**, **21b**, **22a**, **22b**, **23a**, **23b**, **24**, **25**, **26a**, **26b**, **27a**, **27b**, **29a**, **29b**, **30b**

Cover photograph of Yuri and her school friends, reproduced with permission of Debbie Rowe.

Many thanks to Masataka, Ryota, Yuri and their families.

Every effort has been made to contact copyright holders of any material reproduced in this book. Any omissions will be rectified in subsequent printings if notice is given to the publishers.

The paper used to print this book comes from sustainable resources.

Contents

Words appearing in the text in bold, **like this**, are explained in the Glossary.

 Find out more about Japan at www.heinemannexplore.co.uk

Where is Japan?

To learn about Japan we meet three children who live there. Japan is a country in Asia. It is made up of four large islands and about 4000 small ones.

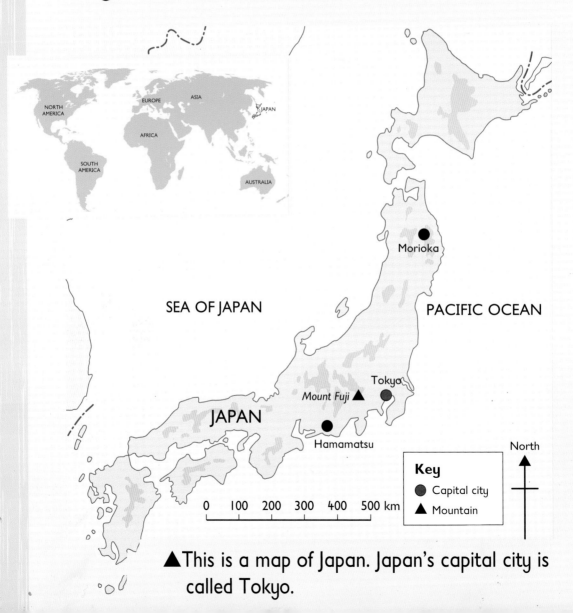

NORTH AMERICA

EUROPE

ASIA

JAPAN

AFRICA

SOUTH AMERICA

AUSTRALIA

Morioka

SEA OF JAPAN

PACIFIC OCEAN

Tokyo

Mount Fuji ▲

JAPAN

Hamamatsu

North

0   100   200   300   400   500 km

Key
● Capital city
▲ Mountain

▲This is a map of Japan. Japan's capital city is called Tokyo.

Japan has lots of high mountains. It is snowy and cold in winter, and hot and steamy in summer.

▲ Mount Fuji is the highest mountain in Japan.

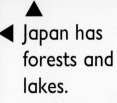

▲
◀ Japan has forests and lakes.

Meet Masataka

Masataka is seven years old. He comes from Tokyo, Japan's capital city. Masataka lives with his parents and his two younger sisters.

Masataka

Miromi

Micki

Masataka's mother

▲ Masataka's family live in a flat near a park.

▲ Masataka's father bows a traditional greeting.

Very old Japanese **traditions** are important to Masataka's family. But they also like modern machines. They have a toilet that flushes by itself!

Masataka at school

Masataka goes to school every weekday. School starts at twenty past eight in the morning. It finishes at three o'clock in the afternoon.

Masataka lives near his ▶ school, so he walks there.

At school, Masataka takes off his shoes and puts on slippers. Japanese people do this when they go indoors. In Japan this is a polite thing to do.

There are 40 children ▶ in Masataka's class.

9

After school

Twice a week Masataka has extra lessons after school. Japanese people think that learning is very important.

Masataka goes to a different ▶ school for his extra lessons.

At home, Masataka plays computer games and looks after his pet hamster. He also likes folding paper into animal shapes. This is a **traditional** Japanese art called *origami*.

Train travel

Japan has three very fast trains. The trains take people in and out of Tokyo. They are called bullet trains.

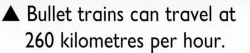

▲ Bullet trains can travel at 260 kilometres per hour.

Over twelve million people live in Tokyo. The city streets are always busy with traffic. So, the quickest way of getting around is to travel on the underground train system.

▼ It can be a squash on the underground!

Meet Ryota

Ryota is seven years old. He lives with his mother and father, his older brother, and his grandmother.

Ryota's father

Takaaki

Ryota's grandmother

Ryota

Ryota's mother

▲ Ryota's parents are both teachers.

Ryota lives in a town called Morioka.
It is in the north of Japan. This area of
Japan has mountains and forests.

Home cooking

It is Ryota's job to lay the table for dinner. **Traditionally** in Japan people eat at a very low table and sit on mats on the floor. Ryota's family use a higher table and chairs.

▼ Ryota's family eat with long **chopsticks**.

chopsticks

Ryota's family eat lots of fish, with vegetables, rice and **noodles**. Ryota's favourite food is fish soup.

◄ This Japanese food is made of rice and raw fish. It is called *sushi*.

Ryota loves sport

Ryota is in a baseball team. Baseball is very popular in Japan. Many families go to watch a baseball game at the weekend.

◀ Ryota wants to be a baseball player when he grows up.

18

Ryota likes **traditional** Japanese sports, too. He goes to a club after school to learn **Judo**.

Japanese traditions

These women are wearing **traditional** Japanese clothes and make-up. They are training to be **geishas**. Geishas learn many traditional skills. They even learn a special way to make tea.

Tea houses often have ▶
beautiful gardens
around them.

Tea houses are a Japanese tradition
too. These two friends are bowing to
each other inside a tea house.

Meet Yuri

Yuri is eight years old. She lives with her parents, grandparents, and her two older sisters. They come from an area called Hamamatsu.

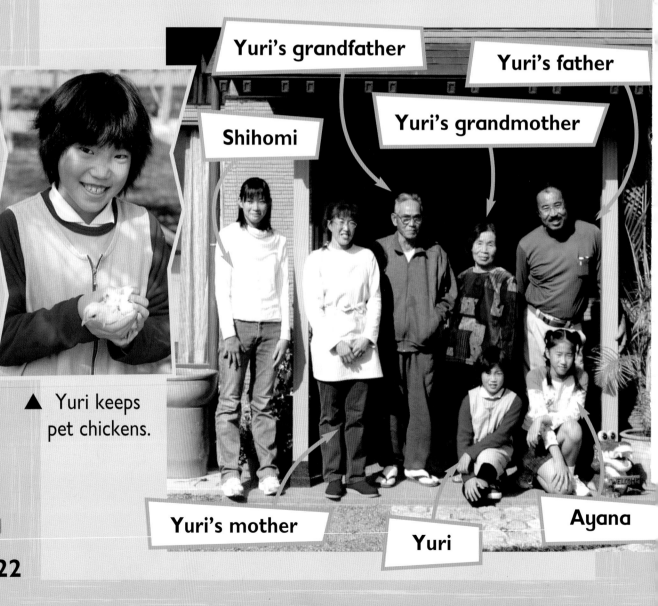

▲ Yuri keeps pet chickens.

Yuri's grandfather

Yuri's father

Yuri's grandmother

Shihomi

Yuri's mother

Yuri

Ayana

Yuri's parents work on a farm. They grow oranges and grapes. Yuri often helps her parents. There are always lots of jobs to be done!

Earthquake practice

Japan sometimes has **earthquakes**. Yuri and her friends take hard yellow hats to school in case an earthquake happens.

hats

Yuri's class often practise what to do
if an earthquake happens. When their
teacher tells them, they hide under
their desks as quickly as they can.

Fun at school

Yuri's favourite lesson is Japanese writing. This is called *kanji*. Japanese writing does not have letters, it has signs. Each sign means a word.

▲ Yuri's *kanji* teacher.

Yuri enjoys serving lunch to the other children. Everyone takes a turn to help with lunch. She also likes it when their homework is to clean the classroom.

Festivals

There are lots of **festivals** in Japan. Some celebrate nature. One festival happens when blossom appears on cherry trees in springtime.

The Seven-Five-Three festival is held in November. Boys who are five, and girls who are three or seven take part. They visit a **temple** to pray for a long, healthy life.

◄ Sometimes people dress up in **traditional** clothes for festivals.

Japanese fact file

Flag	Capital city	Money

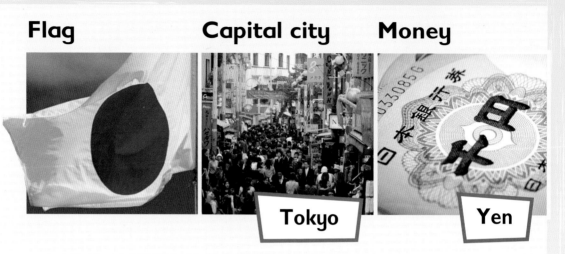

Tokyo

Yen

Religion
• Most Japanese follow Shinto or Buddhism. There are a few Christians too.

Language
• The official language is Japanese.

Try speaking Japanese!

konichiwa .... hello

ogenki desu ka? .... how are you?

doumo arigatou gozaimasu .... thank you

 Find out more about Japan at
www.heinemannexplore.co.uk

Glossary

chopsticks two special sticks used to eat food with instead of knives and forks. They are held in one hand.

earthquake sudden movement of the ground caused by rocks under the earth

festival big celebration for a town or country

geisha Japanese lady trained in traditional Japanese skills, so that she can entertain

Judo old Japanese sport where two people try to throw each other onto the ground

noodles type of long thin, curly pasta

origami special way of folding paper to make animal and flower shapes

temple where people go to pray

tradition something that has been going for a very long time without changing

More books to read

We come from Japan, Teresa Fisher (Hodder and Stoughton, 2002)

Japan, David Marx and Linda Cornwall (Children's Press, 2001)

Index

Titles in the *We're From* series include:

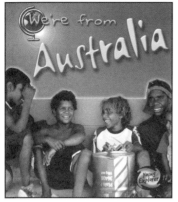

Hardback   0 431 11935 X

Hardback   0 431 11932 5

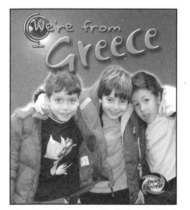

Hardback   0 431 11937 6

Hardback   0 431 11933 3

Hardback   0 431 11936 8

Hardback   0 431 11934 1

Find out about the other titles in this series on our website www.heinemann.co.uk/library